SEJHANE BANUSHI

THE ART OF SELF-MASTERY

THE ART OF SELF-MASTERY

To my daughter,
You are my light and my reason. May this book guide you
to embrace your strength and live with purpose.

EPIGRAPH

"Mastering others is strength. Mastering yourself is true power."
– Lao Tzu

PREFACE

This book began as a deeply personal journey—one that challenged me to understand myself, my strengths, and my limitations. Along the way, I discovered that self-mastery is not a single goal but an ongoing process of growth and alignment. It requires courage, resilience, and, most of all, self-compassion.

In these pages, I share the lessons I've learned, the tools I've developed, and the practices that have transformed my life. My hope is that this book becomes a companion on your path to becoming your best self. Thank you for allowing me to be part of your journey.

ACKNOWLEDGMENTS

This book is the culmination of years of self-reflection, growth, and the desire to create a life of purpose. It represents the beginning of a journey—not just for me, but for everyone seeking mastery over themselves.

To my daughter: You are my light, my teacher, and my constant source of joy. This book began as a dream of leaving something meaningful behind for you—a guide to becoming the best version of yourself. I hope it inspires you as much as you inspire me.

To my readers: Thank you for allowing me into your world. Your willingness to embrace growth is a testament to the power of the human spirit, and I am honored to walk this journey alongside you.

To every struggle, every moment of doubt, and every step for-ward: Thank you for shaping me into the person I needed to become to write this book. This is only the beginning.

DISCLAIMER

This book is intended for informational and inspirational purposes only. It is not a substitute for professional advice, therapy, or medical treatment. The strategies and insights shared are based on the author's personal experiences and research and may not apply to every individual.

Always consult with a qualified professional for specific concerns related to your mental, emotional, or physical well-being. The author and publisher are not responsible for any actions taken or not taken as a result of reading this book.

CONTENTS

THE JOURNEY BEGINS

S elf-mastery is not a destination but a lifelong journey—a deliberate commitment to personal growth and self-awareness.

In a world that often feels chaotic, the ability to master oneself becomes the foundation for peace, purpose, and fulfillment. This book is designed to guide you through the process of taking control of your life, embracing your authentic self, and fostering the resilience necessary to thrive in the face of challenges.

At its core, self-mastery is about understanding who you are and aligning your actions with your highest values and aspirations. It is about learning to navigate your inner world—the thoughts, emotions, and beliefs that shape your reality. By mastering these elements, you unlock the power to shape your external world as well.

What to Expect

Throughout this book, you will find practical strategies, thought-provoking exercises, and actionable insights to help you on your path to self-mastery. Each chapter builds upon the last, offering tools to help you:

- Cultivate deeper self-awareness.
- Overcome fear and self-doubt.
- Build emotional resilience.
- Align your actions with your core values.
- Create habits that support lifelong growth.

The journey of self-mastery is not always easy, but it is deeply rewarding. It requires courage, commitment, and a willingness to face yourself honestly. As you read through these pages, remember that growth is a process, and every step forward—no matter how small—is a victory.

UNDERSTANDING THE POWER OF SELF-AWARENESS

Introduction: The Foundation of Self-Mastery

Self-awareness is the cornerstone of personal growth and self-mastery. It is the ability to see yourself clearly, understand your emotions and behaviors, and recognize how they align with your values and goals. When you cultivate self-awareness, you take the first step toward creating a life of intention, purpose, and authenticity.

This chapter explores why self-awareness is vital, how it impacts every aspect of your life, and the tools and practices you can use to deepen your understanding of yourself.

1.1 Why Self-Awareness Matters

Self-awareness empowers you to:

· Understand your motivations, fears, and desires.

- Recognize patterns in your behavior that support or hinder your growth.
- Strengthen your emotional intelligence by connecting with your feelings.
- Make conscious decisions that align with your long-term goals and values.

Without self-awareness, we act on autopilot, repeating patterns and behaviors that may no longer serve us. By becoming aware of our inner world, we gain the power to change our external circumstances.

Reflection Prompt:
Think about a time when you acted on impulse or emotion. How might self-awareness have changed the outcome?

1.2 The Role of Self-Awareness in Decision-Making
Decisions shape your life, and self-awareness ensures that your choices reflect your values. When you are self-aware, you can pause, reflect, and respond with clarity rather than reacting automatically.

- **Example:** Imagine being in an intense argument. Without self-awareness, you might lash out and escalate the situation. With self-awareness, you can recognize your anger and choose a calm, constructive response.

1.3 Tools for Developing Self-Awareness

1. **Journaling for Reflection**
   Writing is a powerful tool for understanding yourself. By journaling, you can process your thoughts, emotions, and experiences in a structured way.

Exercise: Write a daily self-reflection entry. Include:

- What went well today?
- What did not go as planned?
- How did I feel during key moments of the day?

Over time, review your journal to identify patterns in your emotions and behaviors.

1. **Mindfulness Practice**
   Mindfulness involves observing your thoughts and feelings without judgment. It helps you stay present and become more attuned to your inner world.

Exercise: Spend 5–10 minutes each day practicing mindfulness. Focus on your breath, notice your thoughts as they arise, and let them pass without clinging to them.

1. **Seeking Feedback from Others**
   Sometimes, others can see things about us that we miss. Constructive feedback helps us identify blind spots and gain a fuller understanding of ourselves.

Exercise: Ask someone you trust

- What do you think are my greatest strengths?
- What do you think I could work on?

Listen without defensiveness and reflect on their input.

1.4 Identifying Your Emotional Triggers

Emotional triggers are reactions tied to past experiences or unresolved feelings. Recognizing them is essential for self-awareness.

Reflection Prompt:
What situations consistently evoke strong emotional reactions in you? Are there patterns or themes?

Exercise:
Over the next week, note moments when you feel a strong emotional reaction. Record the situation, your feelings, and your response. At the end of the week, review your notes to identify recurring triggers.

1.5 Overcoming Barriers to Self-Awareness

Self-awareness requires honesty and vulnerability, but common barriers include:

- **Self-Judgment:** Criticizing yourself harshly instead of observing your thoughts with compassion.
- **Avoidance:** Ignoring uncomfortable emotions or truths about yourself.

Strategies for Overcoming These Barriers:

- Practice self-compassion. Remind yourself that self-awareness is about growth, not perfection.
- Create a safe space for reflection, free from distractions or judgment.

1.6 The Benefits of Self-Awareness

When you develop self-awareness, you gain:

- **Improved Relationships:** Understanding yourself helps you communicate and connect with others more authentically.
- **Greater Emotional Resilience:** You can navigate challenges with clarity and composure.
- **Alignment with Your Goals:** Self-awareness helps you identify what truly matters and focuses your energy on it.

Summary

Self-awareness is a journey, not a destination. It requires patience, practice, and a willingness to explore your inner world. Start small—commit to one exercise or tool from this chapter and build from there.

Affirmation:

"I embrace self-awareness as the foundation of my personal growth. I am committed to understanding myself and living authentically."

CHAPTER

2

EMBRACING YOUR AUTHENTIC SELF

Introduction: Living Authentically

To embrace your authentic self is to live in alignment with your true nature, values, and passions. Authenticity is about being unapologetically yourself, free from the constraints of societal expectations or self-imposed limitations. In this chapter, we explore how to discover, accept, and express your authentic self while cultivating the confidence to live authentically.

2.1 Discovering Your True Self

Your authentic self is the essence of who you are when all external influences are stripped away. Discovering this essence requires introspection and a willingness to confront any fears or doubts that may arise.

Reflection Prompt:

Think about moments when you felt most alive and true to yourself. What were you doing? How did it feel?

Exercise: The Self-Discovery Journal

1. Write about your core values, passions, and dreams.
2. Reflect on any area of your life where you feel disconnected from your true self.
3. Set an intention to align your daily actions with your values and passions.

2.2 Breaking Free from External Expectations

Societal norms, cultural pressures, and the opinions of others can cloud your sense of self. Living authentically requires breaking free from these external influences and prioritizing your inner truth.

Exercise: The Expectations Audit

1. List areas of your life where you feel constrained by external expectations (e.g., career, relationships, appearance).
2. For each area, ask yourself, "Whose expectations am I trying to meet?" and "What do I truly want?"
3. Identify one slight change you can make to align more closely with your desires.

2.3 Embracing Vulnerability

Vulnerability is the willingness to show up as you are, even when it feels uncomfortable or risky. It is a key aspect of authenticity, fostering deeper connections with yourself and others.

Exercise: The Vulnerability Practice

1. Identify a situation where you typically hold back due to fear of judgment or rejection.

2. Take a small step toward vulnerability in this situation—such as sharing a thought or feeling you usually keep hidden.
3. Reflect on how this act of openness impacts your sense of self and your connection with others.

2.4 Owning Your Unique Identity

Your uniqueness is your strength. Embracing what makes you different allows you to express yourself authentically and attract experiences and relationships that align with your true self.

Exercise: The Identity Affirmation

1. Write down five qualities, passions, or values that make you uniquely you.
2. Create an affirmation that embodies your identity, such as "I am a creative, compassionate, and resilient individual."
3. Repeat this affirmation daily to reinforce self-acceptance and confidence.

2.5 Navigating Fear and Self-Doubt

Fear and self-doubt often surface when stepping into authenticity. These emotions are natural but must not dictate your actions. By confronting and reframing them, you build the courage to live authentically.

Exercise: The Fear Journal

1. When you experience fear or doubt, write down the specific thoughts and beliefs fueling these emotions.
2. Challenge these beliefs by reflecting on past experiences where you overcame similar fears.
3. Replace them with affirmations of courage and self-trust.

2.6 Building a Life Aligned with Your Authentic Self

Living authentically means making decisions and creating a lifestyle that reflects your true self. It involves aligning your career, relationships, and daily routines with your core values.

Exercise: The Life Alignment Vision

1. Visualize your ideal life, considering your career, relationships, lifestyle, and creative pursuits.
2. Write down specific changes you can make to bring your current life closer to this vision.
3. Break these changes into actionable steps and start implementing them.

Summary

Living authentically is an ongoing journey of self-discovery, courage, and self-acceptance. By embracing your uniqueness, expressing your truth, and aligning your life with your core values, you create a fulfilling and empowered existence.

Affirmation:

"I honor and embrace my authentic self, trusting that my uniqueness is my greatest strength."

OVERCOMING FEAR AND LIMITING BELIEFS

Introduction: **Transforming Barriers into Opportunities**

Fear and limiting beliefs are among the greatest obstacles to self-mastery. They can prevent you from taking risks, pursuing your passions, or fully embracing your potential. However, these barriers can also be transformed into opportunities for growth and empowerment. In this chapter, we explore practical strategies to confront your fears, challenge limiting beliefs, and harness them as tools for personal development.

3.1 Understanding Fear: A Natural Response

Fear is a natural response to perceived threats. While it serves to protect you, it can also hold you back when it arises from imagined dangers or outdated beliefs. To overcome fear, it is crucial to understand its origins and distinguish between helpful and harmful fear.

Reflection Prompt:

Think of a recent situation where fear held you back. Was this fear protecting you, or was it limiting your growth?

Exercise - Fear Inventory:

1. Write down a list of fears that are currently affecting your decisions or actions.
2. For each fear, note whether it is based on a real threat or an imagined one.
3. Identify one small action you can take to face each fear, starting with the least intimidating one.

3.2 Identifying and Challenging Limiting Beliefs

Limiting beliefs are deeply ingrained thoughts that restrict your potential. They often stem from past experiences, societal conditioning, or self-doubt.

Common Examples of Limiting Beliefs:

- "I'm not good enough."
- "I don't have enough time/resources."
- "I always fail when I try something new."

Exercise - Belief Reframing:

1. Identify a recurring limiting belief you hold.
2. Write down evidence that contradicts this belief (e.g., past successes or positive feedback).
3. Replace the limiting belief with an empowering statement, such as "I am capable of learning and growing through challenges."

3.3 The Role of Self-Talk in Overcoming Fear

Your inner dialogue has a profound impact on how you perceive fear and limiting beliefs. Negative self-talk reinforces fear, while positive affirmations help reframe your mindset.

Exercise - Affirming Confidence:

1. Create a list of affirmations that counteract your fears (e.g., "I am brave and resilient," "I trust myself to handle challenges").
2. Repeat these affirmations daily, particularly when fear or doubt arises.

3.4 Reframing Fear as a Catalyst for Growth

Instead of viewing fear as an obstacle, see it as an indicator of areas where growth is possible. Often, what you fear the most is where you have the greatest potential to evolve.

Reflection Prompt:

What opportunities might arise if you moved through your fear instead of avoiding it?

Exercise - Fear Reframe:

1. Choose a specific fear and write down how facing it could benefit you.
2. Break the challenge into smaller, manageable steps and take the first step toward addressing it.

3.5 Tools for Navigating Fear

1. **Visualization:** Imagine yourself successfully navigating the situation that triggers your fear. Picture how it feels to overcome it.
2. **Breathing Techniques:** Practice deep breathing exercises to calm your nervous system when fear arises.
3. **Support Network:** Share your fears with a trusted friend or mentor who can offer perspective and encouragement.

3.6 Letting Go of Fear and Embracing Courage

Letting go of fear is not about eliminating it but learning to act despite it. Courage grows with practice and helps you build resilience over time.

Exercise - Courage Journal:

1. Keep a journal of moments when you faced your fears and the outcomes of those actions.
2. Reflect on what you learned from each experience and how it contributed to your growth.

Summary

Overcoming fear and limiting beliefs is an essential step on the path to self-mastery. By confronting your fears, reframing your beliefs, and taking consistent action, you unlock new possibilities for growth and fulfillment.

Affirmation:

"I release my fears and limiting beliefs, trusting in my ability to grow through every challenge."

BUILDING EMOTIONAL RESILIENCE

Introduction: The Power of Emotional Resilience

Emotional resilience is the ability to bounce back from life's challenges with strength and grace. It is not about avoiding difficult emotions but learning to navigate them with awareness and acceptance. This chapter explores practical strategies to cultivate emotional resilience and thrive in the face of adversity.

4.1 Understanding Emotional Resilience

Emotional resilience allows you to face stress, loss, and setbacks without being overwhelmed. It is a skill that can be developed through intentional practices and a mindset of growth.

Reflection Prompt:

Think about a challenging time in your life. What helped you cope, and what could have made you more resilient?

4.2 The Role of Emotional Awareness

Awareness of your emotions is the first step to building resilience. By recognizing and naming your feelings, you gain the power to respond thoughtfully rather than reacting impulsively.

Exercise – The Emotional Awareness Journal:

- At the end of each day, reflect on the emotions you experienced.
- Write down what triggered each emotion and how you responded.
- Over time, identify patterns and areas for improvement in managing emotions.

4.3 Strategies for Strengthening Emotional Resilience

1. **Practicing Self-Compassion:**
   Treat yourself with kindness when facing challenges. Avoid harsh self-criticism and focus on your efforts and intentions.
2. **Reframing Challenges:**
   Instead of viewing difficulties as setbacks, see them as opportunities to learn and grow.
3. **Cultivating a Support System:**
   Surround yourself with people who uplift and support you.

Exercise – The Resilience Map:

- Draw a map of your personal resources for resilience, including supportive relationships, self-care practices, and coping strategies.
- Keep this map as a visual reminder of your strengths and tools during tough times.

4.4 The Importance of Rest and Recovery

Rest and recovery are essential for maintaining emotional resilience. Overworking or neglecting self-care can lead to burnout and diminished capacity to cope with stress.

Exercise - The Recovery Plan:

- Create a plan for incorporating regular rest and self-care into your schedule.
- Include activities that replenish your energy, such as meditation, nature walks, or creative hobbies.

4.5 Navigating Setbacks with Grace

Setbacks are inevitable, but how you respond to them determines their impact on your growth. Embrace setbacks as a natural part of life and an opportunity to build resilience.

Exercise – Reframing Setbacks:

- Reflect on a recent setback.
- Write down what you learned from the experience and how it contributed to your growth.

Use this exercise to shift your focus from loss to learning.

Summary

Building emotional resilience empowers you to navigate life's challenges with strength and grace. By cultivating self-awareness, self-compassion, and a supportive environment, you can thrive even in challenging times.

Affirmation:

"I am resilient and capable of navigating life's challenges with strength and grace."

THE MIND-BODY CONNECTION

Introduction: **Bridging the Gap Between Mind and Body**

The mind and body are deeply interconnected, influencing each other in profound ways. By understanding and nurturing this connection, you can enhance your overall well-being, emotional resilience, and personal growth. This chapter explores how mental and physical health are linked and provides tools to strengthen the harmony between the two.

5.1 Understanding the Mind-Body Connection

Your thoughts, emotions, and physical state are intertwined. Stress, for example, can manifest as tension in the body, while physical activity can boost mental clarity and emotional stability.

Reflection Prompt:

Think about a time when your physical health affected your mental state or vice versa. How did addressing one aspect improve the other?

5.2 Cultivating Physical Awareness

Becoming attuned to your body's signals is essential for maintaining balance. When you listen to your body, you can identify areas of tension, fatigue, or imbalance and address them proactively.

Exercise - Body Scan Meditation:

1. Find a quiet place to sit or lie down.
2. Close your eyes and take a few deep breaths.
3. Slowly bring your awareness to various parts of your body, starting from your toes and moving upward. Notice any sensations, tension, or discomfort without judgment.
4. Use this practice regularly to cultivate a deeper connection with your physical self.

5.3 Using Movement to Support Mental Health

Physical activity is a powerful tool for improving mental well-being. It releases endorphins, reduces stress, and enhances cognitive function.

Exercise - Movement for Mood:

1. Identify a form of movement you enjoy, such as walking, yoga, dancing, or strength training.
2. Commit to engaging in this activity for at least 20–30 minutes a few times a week.
3. Reflect on how you feel before and after each session, noting changes in your mood or mental clarity.

5.4 Nutrition and Its Impact on the Mind

What you eat significantly affects your mental and emotional state. A diet rich in whole foods, healthy fats, and nutrients supports brain health and emotional stability.

Practical Tips:

- Incorporate foods rich in omega-3 fatty acids, antioxidants, and fiber.
- Stay hydrated, as even mild dehydration can affect mood and focus.
- Limit processed foods and sugars, which can lead to energy crashes and mood swings.

5.5 Breathwork for Mental and Physical Balance

Breathwork is a simple yet effective practice for calming the mind and body. By focusing on your breath, you activate the parasympathetic nervous system, reducing stress and promoting relaxation.

Exercise - Deep Breathing Technique:

1. Sit or lie down in a comfortable position.
2. Inhale deeply through your nose for a count of four.
3. Hold your breath for a count of four.
4. Exhale slowly through your mouth for a count of six.
5. Repeat for 5–10 minutes, noticing how your body and mind respond.

5.6 Aligning Actions with Your Body's Needs

Living in harmony with your body involves aligning your actions with its natural rhythms. This includes getting adequate rest, practicing self-care, and recognizing when to push forward or slow down.

Reflection Prompt:

What is one way you can better honor your body's needs in your daily life?

Summary

The mind-body connection is a cornerstone of self-mastery. By nurturing this relationship through awareness, movement, nutrition, and breathwork, you create a solid foundation for holistic well-being.

Affirmation:

"I honor the connection between my mind and body, nurturing both with care and intention."

SETTING CLEAR AND POWERFUL INTENTIONS

Introduction: The Strength of Intentions

Intention is a powerful force that drives your actions and shapes your reality. It is more than a wish or a goal—it is a deliberate choice to focus your energy on what you want to create in your life. This chapter will guide you through setting intentions that are clear, aligned with your values, and supported by focused actions

6.1 The Nature of Intention

Intentions function as the seed from which every decision and outcome grows. When you set an intention, you declare your desires and direct your focus toward them.

Reflection Prompt:

What are the key intentions guiding your life right now? How do they influence your daily thoughts and behaviors?

6.2 Setting Clear Intentions

Clear intentions are specific, rooted in your values, and aligned with your authentic self. They are more than vague wishes—they are purposeful commitments to action.

Exercise: Crafting Intentions

1. Choose an area of life you want to transform (e.g., career, relationships, health).
2. Close your eyes and take deep breaths, reflecting on what you truly desire.
3. Write your intention in affirmative language (e.g., "I intend to foster meaningful relationships" or "I am creating a thriving career").
4. Place your intention where you can see it daily, as a reminder of your focus.

6.3 The Power of Focus

Focus amplifies the energy of your intentions, transforming them into reality. A scattered mind weakens your power, but a focused mind sharpens your ability to achieve.

Exercise: Mindfulness of Focus

- Throughout the day, redirect your attention to your chosen intention whenever distractions arise.
- Ask yourself, "Does this action align with my intention?"

The Power of One:

- Choose one intention to focus on for 30 days. Take specific actions aligned with it daily and reflect on your progress at the end of each week.

6.4 Aligning Actions with Intentions

Intentions without action remain ideas. To bring them to life, align your choices and behaviors with your goals.

Exercise: Action Planning

1. Break down your intention into smaller, actionable steps.
2. Schedule these actions on your calendar, ensuring consistency and accountability.
3. Track your progress and celebrate milestones.

6.5 Overcoming Challenges and Resistance

Fear and doubt often arise when pursuing intentions. These feelings are natural but must not deter your progress.

Exercise: Releasing Resistance

- Write down any doubts or fears associated with your intention.
- Counter each one with empowering affirmations (e.g., "I am capable of achieving my goals").
- Symbolically release resistance through visualization or a letting-go ritual.

Summary

Setting clear and powerful intentions is a foundational practice for self-mastery. By focusing your energy, aligning your actions, and overcoming resistance, you create a pathway to manifest your desires.

Affirmation:

"I set clear and powerful intentions, aligning my thoughts, actions, and energy to create a life of purpose and fulfillment."

CREATING A GROWTH MINDSET

Introduction: Embracing Growth

A growth mindset—the belief that abilities, intelligence, and talents can be developed through effort and learning—is foundational to self-mastery. It empowers you to view challenges as opportunities and setbacks as lessons. This chapter explores how to cultivate and maintain a growth mindset to unlock your potential and thrive in all areas of life.

7.1 Understanding the Growth Mindset

The growth mindset contrasts with a fixed mindset, where people believe their abilities are static and unchangeable. By shifting to a growth mindset, you embrace learning and resilience, allowing you to achieve more than you thought possible.

Reflection Prompt:

What is one area of your life where you may have a fixed mindset? How might adopting a growth mindset change your perspective?

7.2 Key Principles of a Growth Mindset

1. **Embracing Challenges:** View obstacles as opportunities to gain experience rather than threats to avoid.
2. **Learning from Feedback:** Treat constructive criticism as valuable input for improvement.
3. **Celebrating Effort:** Recognize and reward the process of learning, not just the outcome.

Exercise - Shifting Perspectives:

1. Think of a recent challenge or setback.
2. Reflect on how you responded and what you learned.
3. Write down a reframed perspective: How could this experience help you grow?

7.3 Developing Resilience Through a Growth Mindset

Resilience and a growth mindset go hand in hand. When you face difficulties, a growth mindset helps you persevere and adapt.

Exercise - Resilience Journal:

1. Create a journal entry for challenges you have overcome.
2. Highlight the skills and lessons you gained from these experiences.
3. Use this journal to remind yourself of your capacity for growth during future challenges.

7.4 Practicing Curiosity and Lifelong Learning

Curiosity drives a growth mindset by keeping you open to new experiences and ideas. Lifelong learning enriches your perspective and enhances your skills.

Exercise - Exploring New Interests:

1. Identify a topic, skill, or hobby you have always wanted to explore.
2. Dedicate time each week to learning about or practicing this interest.
3. Reflect on how this new experience broadens your perspective.

7.5 Overcoming Fear of Failure

Fear of failure often stems from a fixed mindset. Reframe failure as a steppingstone to success by focusing on what you can learn from the experience.

Exercise - Failure Reframe:

1. Think of a past failure that initially felt discouraging.
2. Write down the lessons and opportunities it provided.
3. Reflect on how it contributed to your growth and resilience.

7.6 Sustaining a Growth Mindset

Maintaining a growth mindset requires consistent effort and self-awareness. Surround yourself with positive influences and practice intentional reflection to reinforce your mindset.

Exercise - Growth Affirmations:

1. Write a list of affirmations that support a growth mindset, such as:

- ◦ "I am always learning and growing."
- ◦ "Challenges help me become stronger."

2. Repeat these affirmations daily to reinforce your belief in growth.

Summary

A growth mindset unlocks your potential by fostering resilience, curiosity, and a love for learning. By embracing challenges, celebrating effort, and reframing failure, you create a foundation for continuous improvement and fulfillment.

Affirmation:

"I embrace a growth mindset, knowing that my abilities and potential expand through effort and learning."

CHAPTER

8

NAVIGATING THROUGH CHANGE AND UNCERTAINTY

Introduction: Embracing Change

Change is a constant in life, bringing both opportunities and challenges. While uncertainty can evoke fear, it also holds the potential for growth and transformation. This chapter explores how to embrace change, navigate uncertainty, and find strength in the unknown.

8.1 Understanding Change as a Growth Opportunity

Change pushes you out of your comfort zone, forcing you to confront fears, adapt, and grow. By reframing change as an opportunity, you unlock its potential to enhance your life.

Reflection Prompt:

Think of a time when a notable change led to personal growth. How did this experience shape who you are today?

8.2 Releasing Resistance to Change

Resistance to change often stems from fear of the unknown. Letting go of resistance involves accepting the reality of change and focusing on its potential benefits.

Exercise - The Release Ritual:

1. Write down what you feel is resistant to changing in your life.
2. Reflect on how holding onto this resistance impacts your well-being.
3. Perform a symbolic release, such as tearing up or burning the paper, while affirming: "I release what no longer serves me."

8.3 Navigating Uncertainty with Mindfulness

Uncertainty can trigger anxiety, but mindfulness helps anchor you in the present moment, reducing fear and fostering clarity.

Exercise - Grounding Meditation:

1. Sit in a quiet place and take deep breaths.
2. Bring your attention to your body and the sensations of the present moment.
3. Acknowledge thoughts of uncertainty without judgment and let them pass, returning focus to your breath.

8.4 Developing Adaptability

Adaptability is the ability to adjust your mindset and approach when circumstances change. It allows you to navigate challenges with resilience and creativity.

Exercise - The Flexibility Check:

1. Reflect on a recent situation that required you to adapt.
2. Identify what helped you adjust and what made it difficult.
3. List three ways you can become more flexible in your thinking and actions.

8.5 Setting Intentions During Transitions

Transitions are opportunities to realign your goals and values. Setting intentions helps guide you through change with clarity and purpose.

Exercise - The Transition Journal:

1. Reflect on the change you are experiencing and ask, "What do I want to create or achieve in this new chapter?"
2. Write down your intentions and review them regularly to stay focused and motivated.

8.6 Seeking Support During Change

Having a support system is vital for navigating uncertainty. Sharing your experiences with trusted individuals provides perspective and encouragement.

Exercise - The Support Network Map:

1. List people or resources you can rely on for support during transitions.
2. Identify one person to reach out to and share your journey with them.

Summary

Change and uncertainty are opportunities for growth and renewal. By embracing the unknown with mindfulness, adaptability, and intention, you cultivate resilience and discover new possibilities.

Affirmation:

"I embrace change with courage and trust in my ability to adapt and grow."

MASTERING SELF-DISCIPLINE

Introduction: The Foundation of Achievement

Self-discipline is the ability to stay focused on your goals and values, even in the face of distractions or challenges. It is a cornerstone of self-mastery, enabling you to take consistent, purposeful actions toward your aspirations. In this chapter, we explore how to cultivate self-discipline, overcome obstacles, and stay committed to your journey.

9.1 Understanding Self-Discipline

Self-discipline is about making choices that align with your long-term goals rather than succumbing to short-term impulses. It requires clarity, commitment, and a strong connection to your "why."

Reflection Prompt:

What is one area of your life where greater self-discipline could help you achieve your goals?

9.2 Strengthening Your "Why"

Your "why" is the reason behind your goals. A clear and compelling "why" strengthens your motivation and helps you stay disciplined when challenges arise.

Exercise - Finding Your Why:

1. Identify a goal that requires self-discipline.
2. Ask yourself, "Why is this goal important to me?"
3. Dig deeper by asking, "What will achieving this goal allow me to experience or become?"
4. Write down your "why" and revisit it regularly to stay inspired.

9.3 Building Habits that Support Self-Discipline

Habits are building blocks of self-discipline. By automating positive behaviors, you reduce the need for constant decision-making and willpower.

Exercise - The Habit Loop:

1. Choose one habit you want to develop.
2. Identify the cue (what triggers the habit), the routine (the habit itself), and the reward (the benefit you gain).
3. Practice this habit consistently, refining the loop as needed.

9.4 Overcoming Temptation and Distractions

Temptations and distractions can derail even the most disciplined individuals. Overcoming them requires awareness and initiative-taking strategies.

Exercise - The Distraction Audit:

1. List common distractions that hinder your self-discipline.

2. For each distraction, identify a strategy to minimize or eliminate it (e.g., turning off notifications, creating a dedicated workspace).
3. Implement these strategies and assess their effectiveness over time.

9.5 Practicing Delayed Gratification

Delayed gratification is the ability to resist immediate rewards in favor of long-term benefits. Cultivating this skill strengthens your self-discipline and resilience

Exercise - The Gratification Pause:

1. When faced with a tempting but unproductive choice, pause and reflect on the long-term consequences.
2. Ask yourself, "Will this decision bring me closer to or further from my goals?"
3. Practice this pause regularly to build your ability to delay gratification.

9.6 Tracking Progress and Celebrating Success

Tracking your progress keeps you accountable and motivated. Celebrating small successes reinforces your commitment to self-discipline.

Exercise - The Progress Journal:

1. Create a journal to record daily or weekly actions aligned with your goals.
2. Reflect on your progress and celebrate milestones, no matter how small.
3. Use this journal to identify areas for improvement and adjust your approach as needed.

Summary

Mastering self-discipline empowers you to take consistent, purposeful action toward your goals. By clarifying your "why," building supportive habits, overcoming distractions, and practicing delayed gratification, you strengthen your ability to stay focused and committed.

Affirmation:

"I am disciplined and dedicated to my goals. Each step I take brings me closer to the life I desire."

THE ART OF LETTING GO

Introduction: Freedom Through Release

Letting go is a powerful act of liberation. It is about releasing what no longer serves your growth—be it beliefs, habits, relationships, or past experiences. By letting go, you create space for new possibilities and align with your highest self. This chapter explores the tools and practices for letting go with grace and courage.

10.1 The Power of Release

Holding onto the past can weigh you down, keeping you from moving forward. Letting go is not about forgetting but about choosing to release attachments that limit your potential.

Reflection Prompt:

What are you currently holding onto that feels heavy or limiting? How might releasing it open up new opportunities for growth?

10.2 Identifying What No Longer Serves You

Awareness is the first step to letting go. Take time to reflect on areas of your life where you feel stuck, drained, or unfulfilled. This could include outdated beliefs, unhealthy habits, or relationships that no longer align with your values.

Exercise - The Release Inventory:

1. Make a list of beliefs, habits, or situations that no longer serve your growth.
2. Next to each item, write down why you are ready to let it go and what you hope to gain by releasing it.

10.3 Embracing the Process of Letting Go

Letting go is a process that requires patience, self-compassion, and trust. It often involves grieving what you are releasing while embracing the freedom that comes with it.

Exercise - The Release Ritual:

1. Write down what you are ready to let go of on a piece of paper.
2. Create a symbolic act of release, such as tearing the paper, burning it (safely), or burying it.
3. As you perform the ritual, affirm: "I release this with love and gratitude, creating space for new growth."

10.4 Overcoming Resistance to Letting Go

Fear and resistance are natural when letting go of the familiar. These feelings stem from uncertainty and attachment but can be overcome with self-awareness and intentional action.

Exercise - Reframing Fear:

1. Identify a fear associated with letting go.
2. Write down how releasing this attachment could positively impact your life.
3. Replace your fear-based thoughts with affirmations of trust and empowerment.

10.5 The Benefits of Letting Go

Letting go opens the door to:

- Greater emotional freedom.
- Renewed energy and focus.
- Opportunities for new growth and experiences.

Reflection Prompt:

What new possibilities could emerge in your life if you fully embraced the art of letting go?

Summary

The art of letting go is a practice of self-liberation and empowerment. By releasing attachments, you create space for growth, renewal, and alignment with your true self.

Affirmation:

"I release all that no longer serves me, creating space for growth and abundance in my life."

FINDING STRENGTH IN VULNERABILITY

Introduction: The Power of Vulnerability

Vulnerability is often seen as a weakness, but it is, in fact, one of the greatest sources of strength and connection. When you allow yourself to be vulnerable, you open the door to authenticity, trust, and deeper relationships with yourself and others. In this chapter, we explore how vulnerability empowers you and how to embrace it without fear.

11.1 Redefining Vulnerability

Vulnerability is not about exposing yourself to harm but about being honest and open about your feelings, fears, and desires. It allows you to step into authenticity and form genuine connections.

Reflection Prompt:

In what areas of your life do you feel most vulnerable? How can embracing these vulnerabilities help you grow?

11.2 Embracing Vulnerability as a Strength

Being vulnerable takes courage. It involves letting go of the need for perfection and control, acknowledging your imperfections, and showing up as you are.

Exercise - The Vulnerability Practice:

1. Identify a relationship or situation where you tend to guard yourself.
2. Take one small step to show up authentically—share a feeling or thought that you usually keep hidden.
3. Observe how this act impacts your connection with others and your sense of self.

11.3 Breaking Free from the Fear of Judgment

The fear of judgment often holds people back from being vulnerable. Letting go of this fear involves recognizing that your worth is not tied to others' opinions.

Exercise - The Judgment Detox:

1. Reflect on a recent instance where fear of judgment kept you from expressing yourself.
2. Write down why the opinions of others do not define your worth.
3. Commit to one action where you prioritize your truth over fear of judgment.

11.4 Cultivating Emotional Resilience Through Vulnerability

Vulnerability does not mean oversharing or being unguarded; it is about allowing yourself to feel and express emotions without suppressing them.

Exercise - The Emotional Check-In:

1. Set aside time daily to reflect on your emotional state. Write down what you are feeling and why.
2. Practice expressing these emotions constructively in a conversation or through creative outlets like writing or art.

11.5 Building Trust Through Vulnerability

Trust is built when people feel safe being themselves. By embracing vulnerability, you create a space where others feel comfortable doing the same.

Exercise - The Trust Builder:

1. Choose a person with whom you want to build deeper trust.
2. Share a personal story or experience that reveals your true self.
3. Invite them to do the same, fostering mutual understanding and connection.

Summary

Vulnerability is not a weakness but a gateway to strength, authenticity, and connection. By embracing your imperfections and expressing your truth, you deepen your relationships and unlock your inner resilience.

Affirmation:

"I embrace vulnerability as a strength, allowing it to deepen my authenticity and connections."

PRACTICING SELF-COMPASSION

Introduction: The Heart of Self-Mastery

Self-compassion is the practice of treating yourself with the same kindness and understanding that you would offer a close friend. It is essential for self-mastery because it fosters resilience, emotional healing, and a positive self-image. In this chapter, we explore the principles of self-compassion, its transformative power, and practical ways to integrate it into your daily life.

12.1 The Three Elements of Self-Compassion

Self-compassion is built on three core elements:

1. **Self-Kindness:** Replacing self-criticism with gentleness and care.
2. **Common Humanity:** Recognizing that struggles and imperfections are part of the shared human experience.
3. **Mindfulness:** Observing your emotions without judgment or over-identifying with them.

Reflection Prompt:

How do you currently treat yourself during moments of failure or difficulty? How might self-compassion change your approach?

12.2 Rewriting Limiting Beliefs

Limiting beliefs often stem from self-criticism and can hold you back from realizing your full potential. Rewriting these beliefs is a powerful act of self-compassion.

Exercise - Limiting Belief Reframe:

1. Identify a recurring negative thought about yourself (e.g., "I'm not good enough").
2. Challenge its validity by asking, "Is this absolutely true?"
3. Replace it with a supportive affirmation (e.g., "I am capable and deserving of growth").

12.3 The Power of Positive Self-Talk

Positive self-talk is a cornerstone of self-compassion. It shapes your inner dialogue, influences your mindset, and supports emotional resilience.

Exercise - Morning Affirmations:

1. Begin each day by writing or saying three affirmations about your strengths and worth (e.g., "I am strong and resourceful," "I am deserving of kindness").
2. Repeat these affirmations throughout the day, especially during moments of doubt or stress.

12.4 Cultivating Emotional Resilience with Self-Compassion

Self-compassion enhances emotional resilience by helping you process emotions in a healthy and constructive way.

Exercise - The Self-Compassion Letter:

1. Write a letter to yourself from the perspective of a kind and understanding friend.
2. Acknowledge your current struggles, offer empathy, and remind yourself of your strengths and resilience.
3. Revisit this letter whenever self-doubt arises.

12.5 Letting Go of Perfectionism

Perfectionism often leads to unnecessary stress and self-criticism. Embracing imperfection is a vital aspect of self-compassion.

Reflection Prompt:

What areas of your life are you striving for perfection? How might letting go of this need improve your well-being?

Exercise - Progress Over Perfection:

1. Identify one area where you tend to seek perfection.
2. Set a goal focused on progress rather than perfection (e.g., "I will practice for 15 minutes, regardless of the outcome").
3. Celebrate small achievements along the way.

Summary

Practicing self-compassion allows you to approach life with kindness, resilience, and a deeper sense of self-worth. By cultivating self-kindness, mindfulness, and acceptance of your imperfections, you empower yourself to navigate challenges with grace and strength.

Affirmation:

"I treat myself with kindness, patience, and compassion, knowing I am worthy of love and understanding."

CULTIVATING POSITIVE RELATIONSHIPS

Introduction: The Power of Connection

Human relationships are a profound source of joy, learning, and growth. Positive relationships support your journey of self-mastery by offering encouragement, feedback, and love. This chapter explores how to foster relationships that uplift and align with your values, focusing on communication, boundaries, and mutual respect.

13.1 Understanding the Types of Relationships

Relationships take various forms—family, friendships, romantic partnerships, and professional connections. Each type serves a unique role in your life, contributing to your personal and emotional well-being.

Reflection Prompt:

Which relationships in your life feel most supportive? Which ones may require nurturing or reevaluation?

13.2 Building Healthy Relationships

Healthy relationships are grounded in respect, trust, and communication. They provide a safe space for vulnerability and mutual support.

Exercise - Relationship Inventory:

1. List key relationships in your life.
2. Evaluate each one based on how it aligns with your values, supports your growth, and respects your boundaries.
3. Identify areas where you can strengthen connections or establish healthier dynamics.

13.3 Setting Healthy Boundaries

Boundaries are essential for maintaining balance and self-respect in relationships. They protect your energy and ensure interactions align with your well-being.

Exercise - Defining Your Boundaries:

1. Reflect on interactions that make you feel uncomfortable or drained.
2. Write down clear boundaries for these situations (e.g., "I need time alone to recharge after work").
3. Share these boundaries respectfully with those involved.

13.4 Nurturing Empathy and Active Listening

Empathy allows you to connect with others on a deeper level, fostering trust and understanding.

Exercise - Empathy Practice:

1. During your next conversation, focus entirely on listening without interruptions.
2. Reflect on what the other person is expressing and validate their feelings.
3. Notice how this practice strengthens your connection.

13.5 Recognizing and Addressing Toxic Relationships

Not all relationships are beneficial. Toxic dynamics, marked by manipulation, disrespect, or negativity, can drain your energy and hinder growth.

Exercise - Releasing Toxic Connections:

1. Identify relationships that consistently feel unhealthy.
2. Reflect on how these relationships impact your well-being.
3. If necessary, set firm boundaries or distance yourself with compassion.

13.6 Cultivating New Connections

Positive relationships do not just happen; they are cultivated. Actively seeking connections with like-minded individuals enriches your life and supports your growth.

Exercise - Expanding Your Circle:

1. Identify qualities you value in relationships.
2. Seek opportunities to meet new people through groups, events, or hobbies.
3. Approach new connections with openness and authenticity.

Summary

Positive relationships are a cornerstone of a fulfilling life. By cultivating connections based on respect, support, and empathy, you create a network that nourishes your growth and well-being.

Affirmation:

"I attract and nurture positive relationships that support my growth and reflect my values."

MANAGING STRESS AND FINDING BALANCE

Introduction: **Achieving Harmony Amid Life's Demands**

Stress is an inevitable part of life, but it does not have to dominate your experience. Balance is not about perfection; it is about creating harmony between different areas of your life. This chapter focuses on strategies to manage stress effectively while fostering a sense of balance and well-being.

14.1 Redefining Balance: What It Means to You

Balance is unique to each individual. It involves aligning your priorities and making space for what matters most in your life.

Reflection Prompt:

What does balance look like for you? Which areas of your life feel out of alignment?

Exercise - Life Balance Assessment:

1. Create a chart with categories such as career, relationships, health, and leisure.
2. Rate your satisfaction with each category on a scale of 1–10.
3. Reflect on areas needing more attention and identify minor changes to realign your focus.

14.2 Cultivating Self-Care as a Foundation

Self-care is essential for managing stress and maintaining balance. It nurtures your physical, emotional, and mental well-being.

Exercise - Self-Care Ritual:

1. List activities that rejuvenate you, such as journaling, meditation, or outdoor walks.
2. Dedicate time to these practices daily or weekly, treating them as non-negotiable.

14.3 Managing Energy, Not Just Time

While time is limited, your energy fluctuates throughout the day. Managing energy ensures that you remain productive and engaged without burnout.

Exercise - The Energy Log:

1. Track your energy levels at various times of the day for one week.
2. Use this information to schedule demanding tasks during high-energy periods and relaxation during low-energy times.

14.4 Setting Boundaries for Balance

Boundaries protect your time, energy, and well-being. They allow you to say no to distractions and yes to what truly matters.

Exercise - Boundary Setting Guide:

1. Identify areas where you feel overstretched.
2. Write specific boundaries to protect your priorities, such as "I will avoid work emails after 7 PM."
3. Communicate these boundaries to others and hold yourself accountable.

14.5 Integrating Work, Relationships, and Growth

Balance involves harmonizing various aspects of life. It is about integrating work, relationships, and personal growth to enrich each other.

Exercise - Life Integration Plan:

1. Reflect on how your career, personal relationships, and hobbies support your growth.
2. Create a plan to align these aspects, such as pursuing a passion project with loved ones.

14.6 Practicing Mindfulness for Stress Management

Mindfulness helps you stay present and calm amid life's chaos. It reduces stress and promotes a sense of peace.

Exercise - The Mindful Pause:

1. Set aside a few minutes daily to focus on your breath and observe your thoughts without judgment.
2. Use mindfulness throughout the day by asking yourself, "What do I need in this moment?"

Summary

Managing stress and achieving balance are ongoing practices that require intention and effort. By cultivating self-care, setting boundaries, and aligning your life with your values, you create a harmonious and fulfilling existence.

Affirmation:

"I honor my well-being by creating balance and managing stress with care and intention."

ALIGNING ACTIONS WITH CORE VALUES

Introduction: Living with Integrity

Core values are the guiding principles that define who you are and how you choose to live your life. When your actions align with your values, you experience a sense of authenticity and fulfillment. This chapter explores how to identify your core values and align your daily actions with them to create a life of purpose and integrity.

15.1 Understanding Core Values

Your core values are the beliefs and ideals that are most important to you. They shape your decisions, behaviors, and interactions with others.

Reflection Prompt:

What moments in your life have brought you the most joy or fulfillment? Which values were present in those moments?

Exercise - Values Inventory:

1. Write a list of values that resonate with you, such as honesty, growth, kindness, creativity, or freedom.
2. Narrow the list down to your top five values that best define who you are.

15.2 Translating Values into Actions

Living in alignment with your values involves turning them into actionable principles. Each value should guide your choices and behaviors.

Exercise - Values in Action:

1. Take each of your top values and write a corresponding action principle.
   - Example: Value: Compassion → Principle: "I will actively seek ways to support and uplift others."
2. Reflect on how you can apply these principles in your daily life.

15.3 Creating a Value-Driven Life Plan

A value-driven life plan ensures that your goals and actions are aligned with what matters most to you.

Exercise - Life Plan Alignment:

1. Write down your current goals and evaluate how they align with your core values.
2. If a goal does not align, consider whether it needs to be revised or replaced with one that better reflects your values.

15.4 Overcoming Misalignment

At times, your actions may drift away from your values due to external pressures or challenges. Recognizing and addressing these moments is key to maintaining integrity.

Exercise – Misalignment Reflection:

1. Reflect on a recent situation where your actions felt out of alignment with your values.
2. Write about what contributed to the misalignment and how you can address it in the future.

15.5 Staying True to Your Values Amid Change

Life changes can challenge your ability to live according to your values. Flexibility and reflection help you stay anchored.

Exercise – Value Adaptation:

1. Reflect on a recent change or transition in your life.
2. Consider how your values can guide you in navigating this new chapter.

Summary

Aligning your actions with your core values creates a foundation of authenticity and purpose. By identifying your values, translating them into principles, and continuously reflecting on your alignment, you cultivate a life of integrity and fulfillment.

Affirmation:

"I live in alignment with my core values, creating a life of authenticity and purpose."

THE POWER OF DAILY HABITS

Introduction: Building a Life of Purpose

Daily habits are the foundation of your long-term goals and personal growth. They are the small, consistent actions that create meaningful progress over time. This chapter explores the power of habits, the science behind habit formation, and how to design daily practices that align with your values and aspirations.

16.1 Understanding the Significance of Habits

Habits determine how you spend your time and energy each day. By aligning your habits with your core values and goals, you create a life of intention and purpose.

Reflection Prompt:

What daily habits currently shape your life? Which ones contribute to your growth, and which might be holding you back?

16.2 The Science of Habit Formation

Habits are formed through repetition and reinforcement. They consist of three components:

1. **Cue:** A trigger that initiates the habit.
2. **Routine:** The behavior or action.
3. **Reward:** The benefit or satisfaction gained from the habit.

Exercise - The Habit Loop Analysis:

1. Identify a current habit (positive or negative) and analyze its cue, routine, and reward.
2. Reflect on how you can modify or replace it to align better with your goals.

16.3 Creating Positive Habits

Positive habits require intentionality and consistency. Start small, focus on one habit at a time, and build momentum.

Exercise - Habit Stacking:

1. Choose a habit you already practice regularly (e.g., brushing your teeth).
2. Attach a new habit to it by saying, "After [existing habit], I will [new habit]."
   - **Example:** After brushing my teeth, I will meditate for two minutes.

16.4 Breaking Negative Habits

Negative habits can hinder your progress. Breaking them requires awareness, willpower, and a clear strategy.

Exercise - The Habit Replacement Strategy:

1. Identify a habit you want to change.
2. Replace it with a positive habit that fulfills the same need.
   - **Example:** Replace scrolling on your phone before bed with reading a book.

16.5 Tracking Your Progress

Tracking helps you stay accountable and motivated. Use tools like journals, apps, or habit trackers to measure your consistency.

Exercise - The Habit Tracker:

1. Create a habit tracker with a simple grid or use an app to monitor your habits daily.
2. Celebrate streaks and reflect on missed days to maintain momentum.

16.6 Adapting Habits to Life Changes

Life changes may disrupt routines, but flexibility helps you maintain habits in new circumstances.

Reflection Prompt:
What strategies can you use to adapt your habits when facing changes in your environment or schedule?

Summary
Daily habits are powerful tools for creating a fulfilling and intentional life. By understanding habit formation, focusing on positive practices, and adapting to change, you harness their potential to support your self-mastery journey.

Affirmation:
"I create and maintain habits that align with my values and support my growth."

CONQUERING NEGATIVE SELF-TALK

Introduction: Rewriting Your Inner Dialogue

Negative self-talk can be one of the most significant barriers to self-mastery. It undermines your confidence, fuels self-doubt, and creates mental roadblocks that limit your potential. However, you have the power to rewrite your inner dialogue and transform negativity into positivity. This chapter provides tools to identify, challenge, and change negative self-talk patterns, empowering you to build a supportive and uplifting mindset.

17.1 Understanding the Impact of Negative Self-Talk

Your inner dialogue shapes your thoughts, emotions, and actions. Negative self-talk can lead to self-criticism, perfectionism, and a fear of failure. By becoming aware of these patterns, you take the first step toward changing them.

Reflection Prompt:
What are some recurring negative thoughts you have about yourself? How do these thoughts affect your emotions and behavior?

17.2 Identifying Negative Thought Patterns
Negative self-talk often follows predictable patterns, such as catastrophizing, labeling, or overgeneralizing. Recognizing these patterns allows you to address them directly.

Exercise - The Thought Awareness Journal:

1. Keep a journal to track your negative thoughts. Write down situations that trigger them, the thoughts themselves, and how they make you feel.
2. Review your entries weekly to identify recurring patterns.

17.3 Challenging Negative Thoughts
Challenging negative self-talk involves questioning its validity and reframing it in a more constructive way.

Exercise - Thought Reframing:

1. For each negative thought, ask:
    - "Is this thought based on facts or assumptions?"
    - "What evidence contradicts this thought?"
    - "What is a more supportive perspective I can adopt?"
2. Write down the new, positive thought and practice repeating it whenever the negative one arises.

17.4 Replacing Negative Self-Talk with Affirmations
Positive affirmations counteract negative self-talk by reinforcing empowering beliefs. Regular practice helps reprogram your subconscious mind.

Exercise - Affirmation Practice:

1. Write a list of affirmations that resonate with your goals and values (e.g., "I am capable," "I deserve success," "I trust myself to make good decisions").
2. Repeat these affirmations daily, particularly during moments of doubt or stress.

17.5 Cultivating Self-Compassion

Self-compassion helps you respond to self-criticism with kindness and understanding. By treating yourself with care, you build resilience and self-acceptance.

Exercise – The Self-Compassion Letter:

1. Write a letter to yourself as if you were comforting a close friend experiencing self-doubt.
2. Include affirming and supportive words that acknowledge your struggles and strengths.
3. Read the letter whenever negative self-talk arises.

17.6 The Role of Gratitude in Shifting Perspective

Gratitude shifts your focus from shortcomings to strengths, helping to counteract negativity.

Exercise - –he Gratitude Journal:

1. Each day, write down three things you are grateful for about yourself or your life.
2. Reflect on how gratitude changes your perspective over time.

Summary

Conquering negative self-talk is a journey of self-awareness, intentionality, and practice. By identifying and challenging unhelpful thoughts, replacing them with affirmations, and cultivating self-compassion and gratitude, you transform your inner dialogue into a source of strength and support.

Affirmation:

"I choose to speak to myself with kindness and positivity, nurturing a mindset of growth and self-love."

TURNING SETBACKS INTO OPPORTUNITIES

Introduction: The Hidden Gift of Challenges

Setbacks are an inevitable part of life, but they also hold the potential for transformation. By reframing challenges as opportunities for growth, you unlock their hidden value and strengthen your resilience. This chapter explores how to navigate setbacks, extract lessons from them, and use them as steppingstones toward success.

18.1 Understanding the Nature of Setbacks

Setbacks are temporary obstacles that assess your patience, perseverance, and critical thinking skills. Rather than defining failure, they provide a chance to reassess, adapt, and grow.

Reflection Prompt:

Think of a recent setback. How did you respond? What did you learn from the experience?

18.2 Reframing Setbacks as Opportunities

Reframing is the practice of shifting your perspective to see setbacks as opportunities for learning and growth.

Exercise - The Silver Lining Journal:

1. Write about a recent challenge or setback.
2. List at least three positive outcomes or lessons that arose from the situation.
3. Reflect on how these insights can guide your future actions.

18.3 Cultivating a Growth Mindset in the Face of Challenges

A growth mindset helps you view obstacles as opportunities to develop new skills and perspectives. It fosters resilience and optimism, even in difficult circumstances.

Exercise - Growth Affirmations:

1. Write affirmations that reinforce your ability to learn and grow (e.g., "I embrace challenges as opportunities to grow stronger").
2. Repeat these affirmations daily to cultivate a positive mindset.

18.4 Developing a Problem-Solving Approach

When faced with a setback, breaking the situation down into manageable steps helps you regain control and find solutions.

Exercise - The Problem-Solving Framework:

1. Define the setback clearly.

2. List potential solutions, no matter how small or unconventional.

3. Choose one solution to implement immediately and evaluate its impact.

4. Repeat this process, iterating as needed until progress is made.

18.5 Learning to Let Go of Perfectionism

Perfectionism often amplifies the pain of setbacks by setting unrealistic expectations. Letting go of perfectionism allows you to embrace progress over perfection.

Reflection Prompt:

What does perfectionism cost you in terms of stress and missed opportunities? How can you shift your focus to progress and growth?

18.6 Building Resilience Through Setbacks

Each setback you overcome builds your resilience and strengthens your ability to face future challenges with courage and confidence.

Exercise – The Resilience Reflection:

1. Reflect on a time when you successfully navigated a setback.

2. Write about the strengths and resources you used to overcome it.

3. Keep this reflection as a reminder of your resilience during future challenges.

Summary

Turning setbacks into opportunities is a powerful practice of self-mastery. By reframing challenges, cultivating a growth mind-set, and focusing on progress, you transform obstacles into stepping-stones for success.

Affirmation:
"I see setbacks as opportunities for growth, using each challenge to strengthen my resilience and wisdom."

CREATING A VISION FOR YOUR LIFE

Introduction: The Importance of Vision
A clear vision acts as a guiding light for your life. It provides direction, inspires action, and helps you align your choices with your long-term goals. Crafting a vision is not about predicting the future but about intentionally shaping it by clarifying what you desire and why it matters. This chapter guides you through the process of creating a compelling life vision and aligning your actions with it.

19.1 Understanding the Role of Vision

A vision represents your ideal life, encompassing your aspirations, values, and purpose. It helps you stay focused and motivated, especially during challenges and transitions.

Reflection Prompt:

What does your ideal life look like in five, ten, or twenty years?

What emotions, experiences, and accomplishments define this vision?

19.2 Defining Your Life Vision

Your life vision should reflect your authentic self and align with your core values. Take time to explore what truly matters to you.

Exercise – Vision Mapping:

1. Divide your life into categories, such as career, relationships, health, personal growth, and contributions to the world.
2. Write down your ideal scenario for each category. Be specific and use vivid, positive language.
3. Reflect on common themes and how they align with your values.

19.3 Turning Your Vision into Action

A vision without action remains a dream. Break your vision into actionable steps and integrate them into your daily life.

Exercise – Vision to Goals:

1. Choose one aspect of your vision to focus on.
2. Create SMART goals (Specific, Measurable, Achievable, Relevant, Time-bound) to bring this part of your vision to life.
3. Develop a timeline and track your progress regularly.

19.4 Using Visualization to Reinforce Your Vision

Visualization helps you connect emotionally with your vision, strengthening your belief in its possibility.

Exercise - Visualization Practice:

1. Set aside 5–10 minutes daily in a quiet space.
2. Close your eyes and imagine yourself living your ideal life. Engage all your senses—what do you see, hear, feel, and smell?
3. Embrace the emotions associated with your vision, such as joy, gratitude, and confidence.

19.5 Staying Aligned with Your Vision

Consistency is key to maintaining alignment with your vision. Regular reflection and adjustment ensure that your actions continue to support your goals.

Exercise – The Weekly Vision Check-In:

1. At the end of each week, review your actions and decisions. Ask yourself:
   - "Did I take steps toward my vision?"
   - "What can I improve next week to stay aligned?"
2. Adjust your plans as needed to stay on track.

Summary

Creating a vision for your life empowers you to live intentionally and purposefully. By defining your ideal future, taking consistent action, and using tools like visualization, you transform your aspirations into reality.

Affirmation:

"My vision guides me to live a life of purpose and fulfillment. I take inspired actions to create the future I desire."

STAYING COMMITTED TO YOUR SELF-MASTERY

Introduction: The Path of Lifelong Growth

Self-mastery is not a destination but an ongoing journey. Staying committed to this path requires dedication, adaptability, and a clear connection to your "why." This chapter offers strategies to maintain focus, overcome plateaus, and sustain your passion for personal growth.

20.1 Reaffirming Your Purpose

Your "why" is the driving force behind your journey of self-mastery. Regularly reconnecting with your purpose reignites your motivation and keeps you aligned with your goals.

Exercise - Purpose Reconnection:

1. Reflect on why you embarked on the journey of self-mastery.

2. Write a short statement summarizing your purpose.
3. Keep this statement visible as a daily reminder of your commitment.

20.2 Setting Realistic Expectations

Self-mastery involves progress, not perfection. Setting realistic expectations prevents frustration and fosters a sustainable approach to growth.

Reflection Prompt:

Are your expectations for growth aligned with your capacity and circumstances? How can you adjust them to be more realistic?

Exercise - Progress Over Perfection:

1. List recent achievements in your self-mastery journey, no matter how small.
2. Celebrate these milestones as proof of your progress.

20.3 Navigating Plateaus

Plateaus are natural in any journey of growth. They offer an opportunity to rest, reflect, and reassess your approach.

Exercise - The Plateau Reflection:

1. Identify an area where you feel stuck or stagnant.
2. Reflect on what may be contributing to the plateau—overwhelm, lack of clarity, or external challenges.
3. Write down one small, actionable step to reignite momentum in this area.

20.4 Building Accountability

Accountability helps you stay consistent and focused. Whether through a mentor, group, or self-tracking, it reinforces your commitment.

Exercise - Accountability Partner:

1. Identify someone you trust who can support your self-mastery journey.
2. Share your goals with them and agree on regular check-ins to discuss progress and challenges.

20.5 Embracing Flexibility and Adaptability

Life is unpredictable, and your journey will require flexibility to navigate unexpected changes. Adaptability ensures that your growth continues, even in shifting circumstances.

Exercise - The Adaptability Journal:

1. Reflect on recent life changes that have impacted your journey.
2. Write about how you adapted and what you learned from the experience.
3. Use these insights to prepare for future changes.

20.6 Finding Joy in the Process

Sustaining your commitment requires finding joy in the journey itself. Celebrate the process of growth rather than fixating solely on outcomes.

Exercise - The Joyful Practice:

1. Identify one practice or activity in your self-mastery journey that brings you joy.

2. Dedicate time to this practice regularly, focusing on the pleasure it brings.

Summary

Staying committed to your self-mastery journey is an act of dedication and love for yourself. By reconnecting with your purpose, embracing flexibility, and celebrating progress, you ensure that your growth remains a fulfilling and lifelong pursuit.

Affirmation:

"I am committed to my self-mastery journey, embracing growth with patience, joy, and purpose."

YOUR SELF-MASTERY ROADMAP

Bringing It All Together

The journey of self-mastery is not a destination but a continuous process of growth, reflection, and alignment with your values. Throughout this book, we have explored various aspects of self-mastery, from building emotional resilience and cultivating positive relationships to setting intentions and embracing change. Now, it is time to integrate these practices into a cohesive roadmap for your ongoing journey.

The Key Pillars of Self-Mastery

1. **Self-Awareness:**

   Begin every step with an honest understanding of who you are and what you value. Self-awareness allows you to navigate life's challenges with clarity and intention.

2. **Emotional Intelligence:**
   Harness the power of your emotions, using them as tools for connection and growth rather than obstacles.

3. **Resilience and Adaptability:**
   Embrace challenges and change as opportunities to evolve, cultivating the strength to bounce back and thrive.

4. **Purposeful Action:**
   Align your actions with your core values and long-term goals, ensuring that each decision supports your authentic self.

5. **Positive Relationships:**
   Surround yourself with supportive, like-minded individuals who inspire and uplift you.

6. **Commitment to Growth:**
   Stay open to learning and evolving, recognizing that self-mastery is a lifelong pursuit.

Creating Your Personalized Roadmap

1. **Reflect Regularly:**
   Set aside time for self-reflection to assess your progress and realign with your goals.

2. **Set Intentions:**
   Define clear intentions for each area of your life and revisit them frequently.

3. **Track Progress:**
   Use tools like journaling or habit trackers to measure your growth and celebrate milestones.

4. **Stay Flexible:**
   Life is dynamic. Be willing to adapt your plans and goals as you gain new insights and face unexpected changes.

5. **Seek Support:**
Build a network of mentors, friends, or communities that align with your journey and offer encouragement.

Looking Forward

The practices outlined in this book are meant to serve as a foundation. Your self-mastery journey will be as unique as you are, shaped by your values, experiences, and aspirations. Embrace it with curiosity, courage, and compassion.

Final Affirmation

"I am committed to my journey of self-mastery, embracing growth, resilience, and authenticity every step of the way."

Glossary

- **Self-Mastery**
  The process of gaining control over your emotions, habits, and thoughts to align with your goals and values.
- **Emotional Resilience**
  The ability to navigate life's challenges with strength and grace, adapting to adversity without losing balance.
- **Growth Mindset**
  A belief that abilities and intelligence can be developed through effort, learning, and perseverance.
- **Mindfulness**
  The practice of being present in the moment, observing thoughts and feelings without judgment.
- **Limiting Beliefs**
  Deeply held thoughts or assumptions that restrict your ability to achieve goals or embrace opportunities.
- **Core Values**
  Fundamental principles or beliefs that guide your decisions and actions, reflecting what matters most to you.
- **Authenticity**
  Living in alignment with your true self, free from societal expectations or self-imposed limitations.
- **Self-Discipline**
  The ability to stay focused and take consistent actions toward your goals, even when motivation wanes.
- **Procrastination**
  The habit of delaying important tasks, often due to fear, overwhelm, or lack of clarity.
- **Vulnerability**
  The willingness to show your true self, including your emotions and imperfections, as a source of strength.

- **Letting Go**
Releasing attachments, habits, or beliefs that no longer serve your growth, to create space for new possibilities.
- **Vision Mapping**
The process of defining your ideal life and setting clear goals to align with that vision.
- **Affirmations**
Positive, empowering statements that reinforce self-belief and help reframe negative thoughts.
- **Habit Loop**
The cycle of cue, routine, and reward that forms the foundation of habits and can be adjusted to support growth.
- **Accountability Partner**
A trusted individual who helps you stay focused and committed to your goals through regular check-ins and support.
- **Self-Reflection**
The practice of introspectively examining your thoughts, actions, and experiences to promote personal growth.
- **Purposeful Action**
Intentional decisions and behaviors aligned with your values and long-term aspirations.

Sejhane Banushi is a writer, linguist, and advocate for personal growth who specializes in helping individuals unlock their full potential through discipline and intentional living. Building on her background in linguistics and communication, Sejhane brings a fresh, relatable approach to self-development.

A proud mother and entrepreneur, Sejhane's work is inspired by her own journey of overcoming challenges and embracing growth. She believes that discipline is not a limitation but a gateway to freedom and fulfillment.

When she's not writing or mentoring, you'll find her exploring creative ventures and supporting others in achieving their dreams.

THANK YOU FOR JOINING THE JOURNEY

Thank you for joining me on this journey toward self-mastery. Your commitment to growth is inspiring, and I hope this book has provided you with tools to unlock your potential.

If this book has impacted you, I'd love to hear about your journey. Consider leaving a review online or sharing your thoughts on social media. Your feedback helps others discover this work and join the path to self-mastery.

Let's stay connected:

- Follow me on Instagram: Sejhane Banushi
- Connect with me on LinkedIn: Sejhane Banushi

This is only the beginning—stay curious, stay committed, and keep mastering yourself.

CLOSING NOTE

Thank you for choosing to embark on this journey of self-mastery. Remember, growth is not a destination but a lifelong process. Be kind to yourself, stay curious, and keep striving for the best version of you. Your journey inspires mine.